Fifty Years of Hits
Volume Two
100 songs arranged for piano, voice & guitar

Wise Publications
part of The Music Sales Group
London/New York/Paris/Sydney/Copenhagen/Berlin/Madrid/Hong Kong/Tokyo

Published by
Wise Publications
14-15 Berners Street,
London W1T 3LJ, UK.

Exclusive Distributors:
Music Sales Limited
Distribution Centre, Newmarket Road,
Bury St Edmunds, Suffolk IP33 3YB, UK.
Music Sales Corporation
180 Madison Avenue, 24th Floor,
New York NY 10016, USA.
Music Sales Pty Limited
Level 4, Lisgar House,
30-32 Carrington Street,
Sydney, NSW 2000, Australia.

Order No. AM1012154
ISBN 978-1-78558-387-2

Compiled by Lisa Cox
Designed by Pearce Marchbank RDI

Printed in the EU

Your Guarantee of Quality
As publishers, we strive to produce every book to
the highest commercial standards. This book has
been carefully designed to minimise awkward
page turns and to make playing from it a real
pleasure. Particular care has been given to
specifying acid-free, neutral-sized paper made
from pulps which have not been elemental
chlorine bleached. This pulp is from farmed
sustainable forests and was produced with
special regard for the environment. Throughout,
the printing and binding have been planned to
ensure a sturdy, attractive publication which
should give years of enjoyment. If your copy fails
to meet our high standards, please inform us
and we will gladly replace it.

www.musicsales.com

Contents by song title

Contents by artist

Christmas Alphabet

Words & Music by Buddy Kaye & Jules Loman

Moderately slow

"C" is for the can-dy trimmed a-round the Christ-mas tree. "H" is for the hap-pi-ness with all the fam-i-ly. "R" is for the rein-deer pranc-ing by the win-dow pane.

From Me To You

Words & Music by John Lennon & Paul McCartney

I Want To Hold Your Hand

Words & Music by John Lennon & Paul McCartney

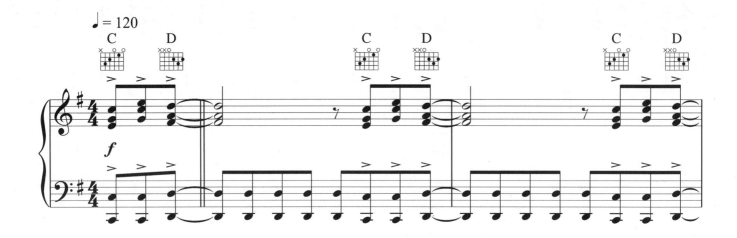

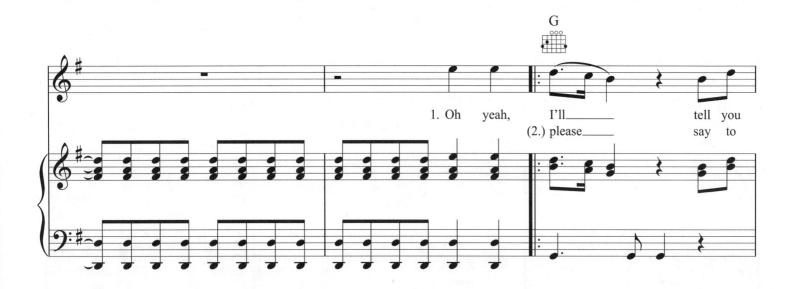

1. Oh yeah, I'll_____ tell you
(2.) please_____ say to

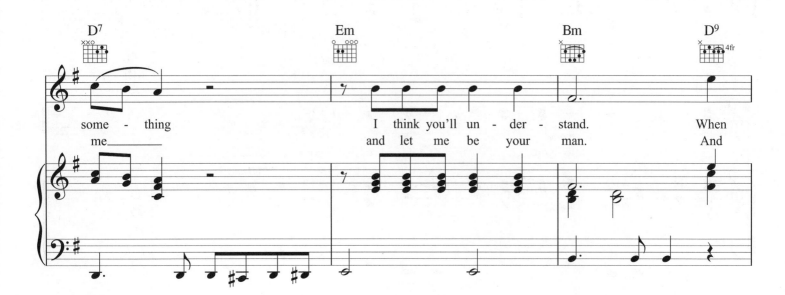

some-thing
me_____

I think you'll un-der-stand.
and let me be your man.

When
And

Eight Days A Week

Words & Music by John Lennon & Paul McCartney

1. Ooh, I need your love, babe,___ guess you know it's true.___
2. Love you ev - 'ry day, girl,___ al - ways on my mind.__

Hope you need my love, babe,___ just like I need you.___
One thing I can say, girl,___ love you all the time.___

Ooh I need your love, babe,___ guess you know it's true.___
Love you ev - 'ry day, girl,___ al - ways on my mind.___

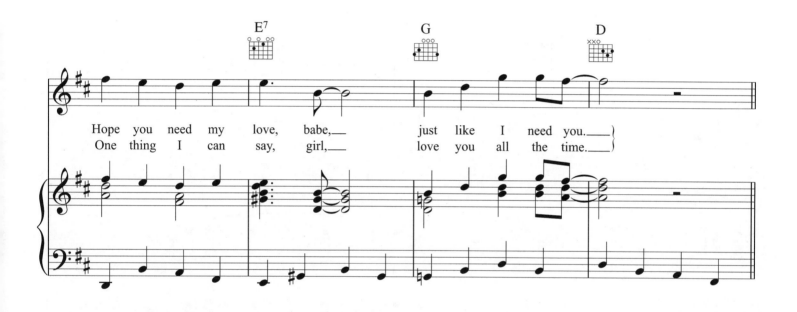

Hope you need my love, babe,___ just like I need you.___
One thing I can say, girl,___ love you all the time.___

Hold me,___ love me,___ hold me,___ love me.___ I

ain't got noth-in' but love, babe,_____ eight days a week._____

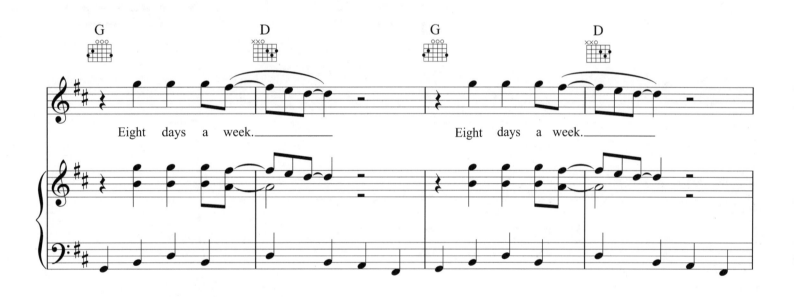

Eight days a week._____ Eight days a week._____

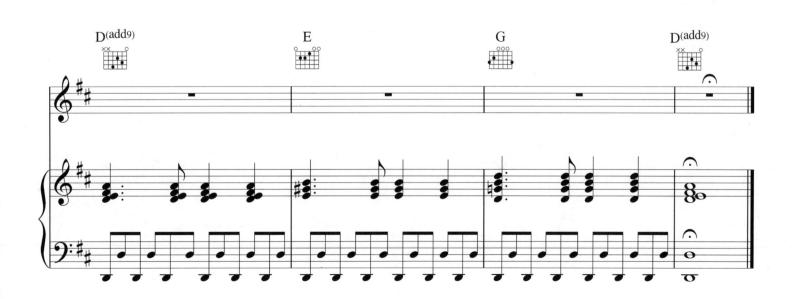

Goldfinger

Words by Leslie Bricusse & Anthony Newley

Music by John Barry

Slowly

Gold - fin - ger   he's the man, the man with the mi - das touch, a spi - der's touch.

Such a cold fin - ger

beck-ons you to en - ter his web of sin

but don't go in.   Gold - en

words he will pour in your ear   but his lies can't dis - guise what you

Day Tripper

Words & Music by John Lennon & Paul McCartney

Moderate Rock

1. Got a good rea - son   for
2. She's a big teas - er,
3. Tried___ to please___ her,

taking the eas - y way out.____
she took me half____ the way there.____
she on - ly played____ one night stands.____

Got a good rea - son
She's a big teas - er,
Tried____ to please____ her,

for tak - ing the eas - y way out,____ now.
she took me half____ the way there,____ now.
she on - ly played____ one night stands,____ now.

She was a
She was a
She was a

Day_____ Trip - per,
Day_____ Trip - per,
Day_____ Trip - per,

one - way tick - et, yeah.____
one - way tick - et, yeah.____
Sun - day driv - er, yeah.____

It took me so_____ long___ to find out_

and I found out.

out.

Michelle

Words & Music by John Lennon & Paul McCartney

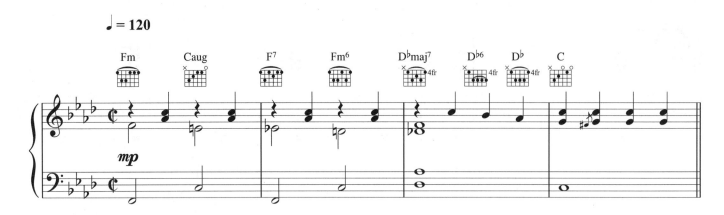

Mi - chelle, ma belle, These are words that go to - geth - er

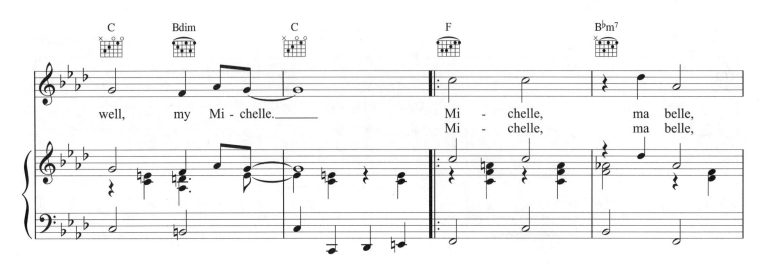

well, my Mi - chelle.

Mi - chelle, ma belle,
Mi - chelle, ma belle,

Ticket To Ride

Words & Music by John Lennon & Paul McCartney

Moderate rock tempo

Help!

Words & Music by John Lennon & Paul McCartney

down,_____ and I do_____ ap - pre - ci - ate_____ you be - ing 'round_

Help me get____ my feet____ back on the ground._

Won't you please, please_____ help___ me?___

1. Help me, help me!_____ **2.** Ooh.

Born Free

Words by Don Black
Music by John Barry

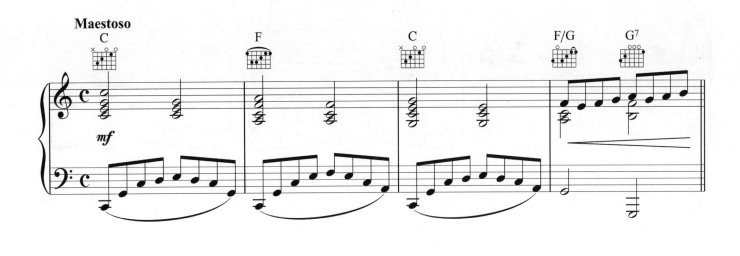

Born free,_____ as free as the wind blows,_____ as free as the

grass grows, born free to fol - low your heart.

Yellow Submarine

Words & Music by John Lennon & Paul McCartney

50

Penny Lane

Words & Music by John Lennon & Paul McCartney

With A Little Help From My Friends

Words & Music by John Lennon & Paul McCartney

Mm, I get high___ with a lit-tle help___ from my friends.___

Mm, I'm gon-na try___ with a lit-tle help___ from my friends.___

I Am The Walrus

Words & Music by John Lennon & Paul McCartney

cry - ing.___

1. Sit - ting on a corn - flake___
2. Yel - low mat - ter cus - tard___
3. Sem - o - li - na pil - chards___

wait - ing for the van to come.___
drip - ping from a dead dog's eye.___
climb - ing up the Eif - fel Tow - er.___

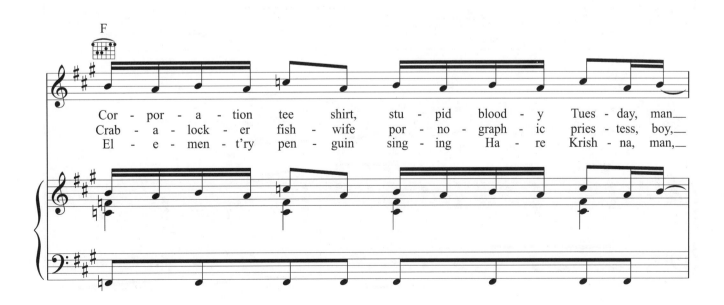

Cor - por - a - tion tee shirt, stu - pid blood - y Tues - day, man___
Crab - a - lock - er fish - wife por - no - graph - ic pries - tess, boy,___
El - e - men - t'ry pen - guin sing - ing Ha - re Krish - na, man,___

64

D.S. al Coda   **⊕ Coda**

Repeat ad lib and fade

wal - rus.   Goo - goo g' joob g' goo___ goo g' joob.   Ex - pert tex - pert chok - ing smok - ers

don't you think the jo - ker laughs at you?_____   See how they smile, like pigs in a sty, see

how they snied.   I'm cry - ing.___   wal - rus.   Goo goo g' joob g' goo___

___ goo g' joob.___   Goo goo g' goo g' goo goo g' joob   joob.   *(Ju - ba ju - ba ju - ba.)*

All You Need Is Love

Words & Music by John Lennon & Paul McCartney

Love, love, love. Love, love, love.

Love, love, love.

1. There's noth-ing you can do that can't be done._____
2. There's noth-ing you can make that can't be made._____
3. There's noth-ing you can know that is-n't known._____

Strawberry Fields Forever

Words & Music by John Lennon & Paul McCartney

3. Al-ways know some-times___ think it's me, but you know I know when it's___ a

dream.___ I think a no will mean a yes but it's all___ wrong,

that is I think I___ dis-a-gree. Let me take you down___'cause I'm go-ing to___

___ Straw-ber-ry Field. Noth-ing is real, and

Hel - la he - ba hel - lo - a. Hel - la he - ba hel -

The Stranger Song

Words & Music by Leonard Cohen

1. It's true that all the men you knew were deal-ers who said they were through, with deal-ing ev-ery time you gave them shel-ter. I know that kind of man, it's hard to hold the hand of

told you when I came I was a stran - ger.   I

Verse 2
And then sweeping up the jokers that he left behind
You find he did not leave you very much
Not even laughter
Like any dealer, he was watching for the card
That is so high and wild
He'll never need to deal another
He was just some Joseph looking for a manger
He was just some Joseph looking for a manger

Verse 3
And then leaning on your window sill
He'll say one day you caused his will
To weaken with your love and warmth and shelter
And then taking from his wallet
An old schedule of trains, he'll say
"I told you when I came I was a stranger
I told you when I came I was a stranger."

Verse 4
But now another stranger
Seems to want to ignore his dreams
As though they were the burden of some other
O, you've seen that kind of man before
His golden arm dispatching cards
But now it's rusted from the elbow to the finger
Yes, he wants to trade the game he knows for shelter

Verse 5
You hate to watch another tired man lay down his hand
Like he was giving up the holy game of poker
And while he talks his dreams to sleep
You notice there's a highway that is
Curling up like smoke above his shoulder
It's curling up like smoke above his shoulder

Verse 6
You tell him to come in, sit down
But something makes you turn around
The door is open, you can't close your shelter
You try the handle of the road
It opens, do not be afaird
It's you, my love, you who are the stranger
It's you, my love, you who are the stranger

Verse 7
Well, I've been waiting, I was sure
We'd meet between the trains we're waiting for
I think it's time to board another
Please understand, I never had a secret chart
To get me to the heart
Of this or any other matter
When he talks like this
You don't know what he's after
When he speaks like this
You don't know what he's after

Verse 8
Let's meet tomorrow, if you choose
Upon the shore, beneath the bridge
That they are building on some endless river
Then he leaves the platform
For the sleeping car that's warm, you realize
He's only advertising one more shelter
And it comes to you, he never was a stranger
And you say, "O.K., the bridge or someplace later"

Verse 9
And then sweeping up the jokers that he left behind
You find he did not leave you very much
Not even laughter
Like any dealer, he was watching for the card
That is so high and wild
He'll never need to deal another
He was just some Joseph looking for a manger
He was just some Joseph looking for a manger

Verse 10
And then leaning on your window sill
He'll say one day you caused his will
To weaken with your love and warmth and shelter
And then taking from his wallet
An old schedule of trains, he'll say
"I told you when I came I was a stranger
I told you when I came I was a stranger."

Blackbird

Words & Music by John Lennon & Paul McCartney

1. Black-bird sing-ing in the dead of night
2. Black-bird sing-ing in the dead of night
(3° instrumental)

Take these bro-ken wings___ and learn to fly;___
Take these sunk-en eyes___ and learn to see;___

all   your life_____ you were on-ly wait-ing for this mo-ment to a-
all   your life_____ you were on-ly wait-ing for this mo-ment to be

Lady Madonna

Words & Music by John Lennon & Paul McCartney

Mon - day's child has learned to tie_____ his boot - lace._____
Thurs - day night your stock - ings need - ed mend - ing._____

See how they run!_____

Because

Words & Music by John Lennon & Paul McCartney

Get Back

Words & Music by John Lennon & Paul McCartney

Jo Jo was a man who thought___ he was a lon-er, but___ he knew it could-n't last.___

to where you once be - longed._____ *Spoken: Get back Jo Jo.*

Go home.

Get back,_____ get back,_____ back_

Oh! Darling

Words & Music by John Lennon & Paul McCartney

In The Ghetto

Words & Music by Mac Davis

Verse 2:
Well the world turns
And a hungry little boy with a runny nose
Plays in the street as a cold wind blows
In the ghetto.
And his hunger burns
So he starts to roam the streets at night
And he learns how to steal and he learns how to fight
In the ghetto.

Verse 3:
His Mama cries
As a crowd gathers round an angry young man
Face down in the street with a gun in his hand
In the ghetto.
And as her young man dies
On a cold and grey Ghicago morning
Another little baby child is born
In the ghetto.

Let It Be

Words & Music by John Lennon & Paul McCartney

Let it be,___ let it be. Let it be,___ ___ yeah,_ let it be.___ Whis-per words_ of wis-dom. Let it be._ Ooh. 3. And

D.S. al Coda

Coda

rit.

A Case Of You

Words & Music by Joni Mitchell

Just be-fore_ our love got lost you said,___ "I am as con-

-stant as a north-ern star",and I said, "Con-stant-ly in the dark — ness, where's that_

you are in my___ blood like ho - - ly wine,___ you taste so bit - ter___

and so sweet.___ Oh, I could drink a case___ of___ you,___

___ dar - ling, and I would still___ be on my feet, oh, I would still be on___

___ my___ feet.___

More Than A Feeling

Words & Music by Tom Scholz

looked out this morn - ing and the sun was gone.__ I turned on some mu - sic to

2. So man - y peo - ple have come and gone.___ Their fac - es fade__ as the years

3. When I'm tired__ and think-ing cold I hide in my mu - sic, for -

D.S. al Coda I

Coda I

slipped a - way._____ *Guitar solo*

She slipped a - way._____

116

117

One Love (People Get Ready)

Words & Music by Bob Marley & Curtis Mayfield

120

Human Nature

Words & Music by Steve Porcaro & John Bettis

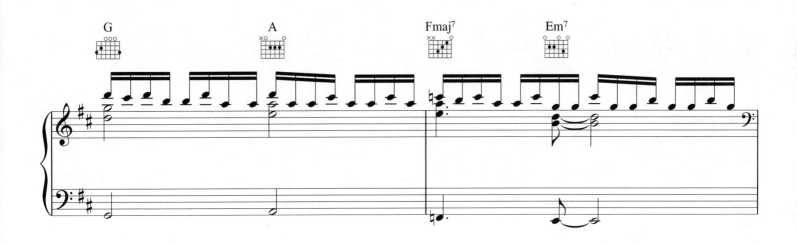

1. Look-ing out__ 'cross__ the night-time, the cit-y winks a sleep-less

(funky 'off-beat' feel throughout)

That way, that way,____

that way, that way.____

Look - ing out___

do me that way? If they— say why, why, da - da - da - da - da - da - da - da,

why, why, why, does he do me that way? I'm like

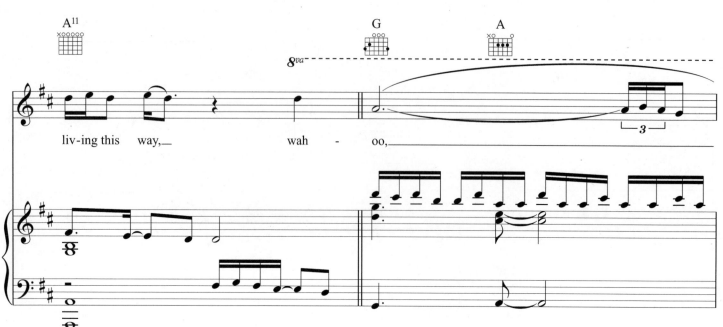

liv-ing this way,— wah - oo,

Repeat to fade

129

Like A Virgin

Words & Music by Tom Kelly & Billy Steinberg

found you. I was beat, in - com - plete.
love can last. You're so fine, and you're mine.
and you're mine.

I'd been had. I was sad and blue. But you
Make me strong. Yeah, you make me bold. Oh, your
I'll be yours till the end of time. 'Cause you

made me feel, yeah, you made me feel
love thawed out, yeah, your love thawed out
made me feel, yeah, you made me feel

next to__ mine.__ Like a vir - gin. Ooh,___ ooh,___ like a

vir - gin. Feels so good_ in - side_____ when you

hold me and your heart beats and you love me. Like a

Repeat to fade

True Colors

Words & Music by Billy Steinberg & Tom Kelly

true col - ors,____ your true col - ors are____

beau - ti - ful____ like a rain - - bow.

D.S. al Coda

Coda *rit.*

Ooh,_____ ooh,_____ ah - ha,_____ ooh.

139

Hallelujah

Words & Music by Leonard Cohen

1. Ba- by, I've been here be- fore; I know this room, I walked this floor. I
(Verses 2-5 see block lyrics)

used to live a - lone_____ be- fore I knew you. Yeah, and I've

seen your flag on the mar-ble arch. But lis-ten, love; love is not some kind of vic-t'ry march. No, it's a cold_

_ and it's a ver-y bro-ken_ hal-le-lu-jah._ Hal-le-

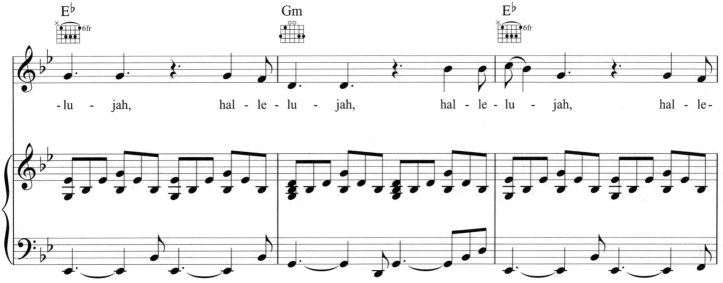

-lu - jah, hal-le-lu-jah, hal-le-lu-jah, hal-le-

-lu - jah, hal - le - lu - - - - - jah.

Verse 2:
There was a time you let me know
What's really going on below
Ah, but now you never show it to me, do you?
Ah, but I remember, yeah, when I moved in you
And the holy dove, she was moving too
Yes, and every single breath that we drew was hallelujah.

Hallelujah, hallelujah, hallelujah, hallelujah.

Verse 3:
Maybe there's a God above
As for me, and all I ever seem to learn from love
Is how to shoot at someone who outdrew you.
Ah, but it's not a complaint that you hear tonight
It's not the laughter of someone who claims to have seen the light
No, it's a cold and it's a very lonely hallelujah.

Hallelujah, hallelujah, hallelujah, hallelujah.

Verse 4:
Instrumental

Hallelujah, hallelujah, hallelujah, hallelujah.

Verse5:
I did my best, it wasn't much
I couldn't feel, so I learned to touch
I've told the truth, I didn't come all this way to fool you.
Yeah, and even though it all went wrong
I'll stand right here before the Lord of Song
With nothing on my tongue but hallelujah.

Hallelujah, hallelujah, hallelujah, hallelujah.
Hallelujah, hallelujah, hallelujah, hallelujah.

Everybody Knows

Words & Music by Leonard Cohen & Sharon Robinson

Moderately, with a steady beat

1. Ev -'ry - bo - dy knows that the dice are
(Verses 4-6 see block lyrics)

*optional quaver note pattern
continues throughout*

load - ed. Ev -'ry - bo - dy rolls with their fin - gers crossed. Ev -'ry - bo - dy

Verse 4:

And everybody knows that it's now or never.
Everybody know that it's me or you.
And everybody knows that you live forever
When you've done a line or two.
Everybody knows the deal is rotten:
Old Black Joe's still pickin' cotton
For your ribbons and bows. And everybody knows.

Verse 5:

Everybody knows that the plague is coming.
Everybody knows that it's moving fast.
Everybody knows that the naked man and woman
Are just a shining artifact of the past.
Everybody knows the scene is dead,
But there's gonna be a meter on your bed
That will disclose what everybody knows.

Verse 6:

And everybody know that you're in trouble.
Everybody knows what you've been through,
From the bloody cross on top of Calvary
To the beach of Malibu.
Everybody knows it's coming apart:
Take one last look at this Sacred Heart
Before it blows. And everybody knows.

Eternal Flame

Words & Music by Susanna Hoffs, Tom Kelly & Billy Steinberg

154

Tower Of Song

Words & Music by Leonard Cohen

Moderately, with a steady beat

1. Well, my friends are gone and my hair is grey.
(Verses 2-5 see block lyrics)

I ache in the pla - ces where I used to play. And I'm cra - zy for love,

but I'm not com - ing on.
I'm just

pay - ing my rent ev - 'ry day in the To - wer of Song.___

1, 2.
3, 4.
5.

2. I
3. I was

4. So you can
5. Now you can

I see you stand - ing on the oth - er side.___ I don't know how the ri - ver

157

never have to lose it again._____ Now I bid you farewell,_____ I don't know when I'll be back._____ They're moving us tomorrow to that tower down the track. But you'll be hearing from me, baby, long after I'm gone.

Verse 2:

I said to Hank Williams, "How lonely does it get?"
Hank Williams hasn't answered yet.
But I hear him coughing all night long,
A hundred floors above me in the Tower of Song.

Verse 3:

I was born like this, I had no choice.
I was born with the gift of a golden voice.
And twenty-seven angels from the Great Beyond,
They tied me to this table right here in the Tower of Song.

Verse 4:

So you can stick your little pins in that voodoo doll.
I'm very sorry, baby, doesn't look like me at all.
I'm standing by the window where the light is strong.
They don't let a woman kill you, not in the Tower of Song.

Verse 5:

Now you can say that I've grown bitter, but of this you may be sure:
The rich have got their channels in the bedrooms of the poor.
And there's a mighty judgement coming, but I may be wrong.
You see, you hear these funny voices in the Tower of Song.

Licence To Kill

**Words & Music by John Barry, Leslie Bricusse, Anthony Newley, Narada Michael Walden,
Walter Afanasieff & Jeffrey Cohen**

please, I need, I've got to hold on to your love. Ooh.

1. Hey, ba - by, thought you were the one who tried to run a -
2. Hey, ba - by, think you need a friend to stand up by your

- way.
side.

Ooh, ba - by,
Ooh, ba - by,

was - n't I the one who made you want to stay?
now you can de - pend on me to keep things right.

Please don't

Jealousy

Words & Music by Neil Tennant & Chris Lowe

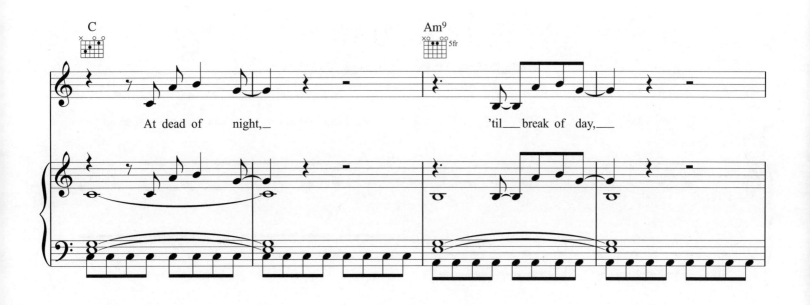

At dead of night,__ 'til__ break of day,__

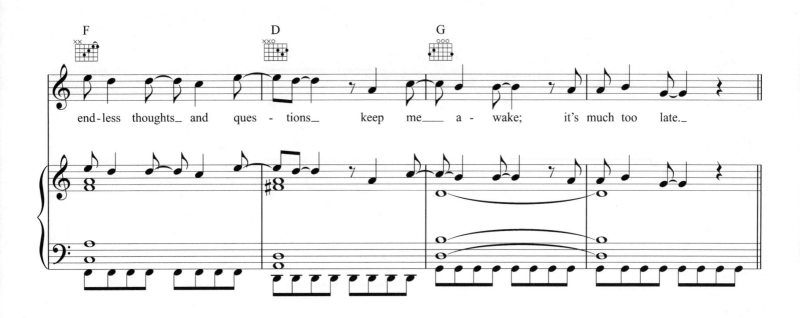

end-less thoughts__ and ques - tions__ keep me__ a - wake; it's much too late.__

Where've you been? Who've you seen? You did - n't phone when you said you would.

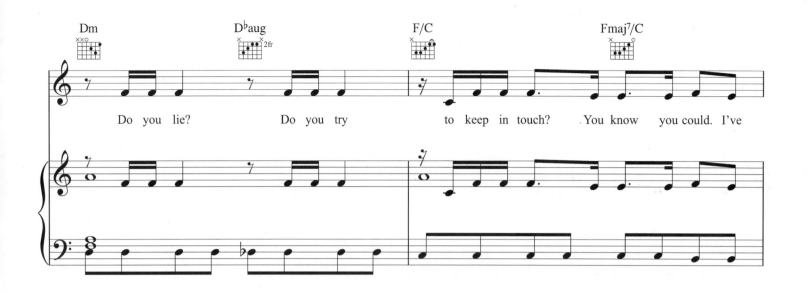

Do you lie? Do you try to keep in touch? You know you could. I've

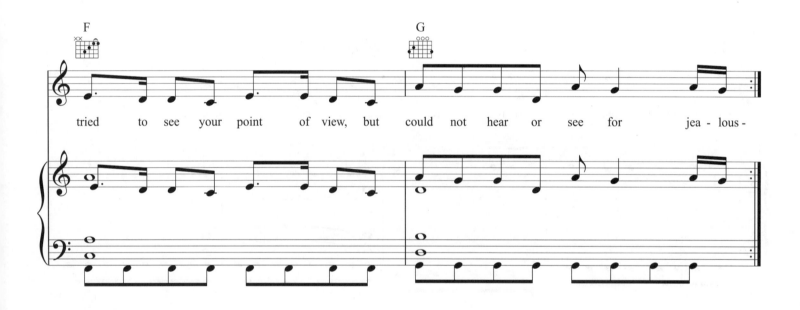

tried to see your point of view, but could not hear or see for jea-lous-

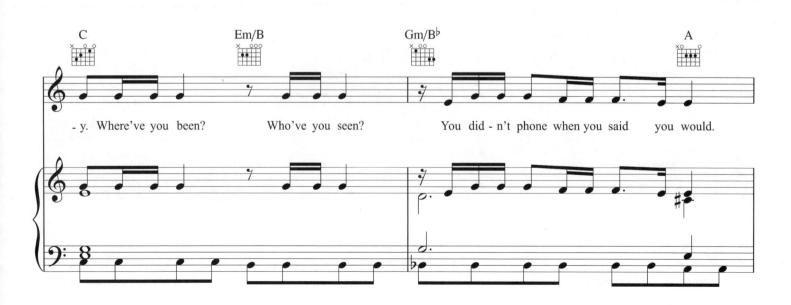

-y. Where've you been? Who've you seen? You did-n't phone when you said you would.

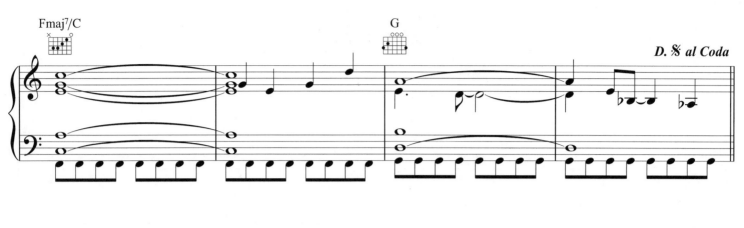

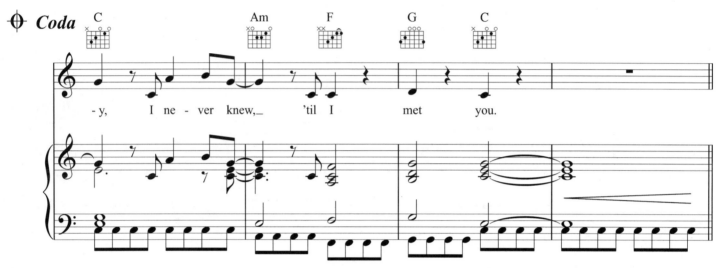

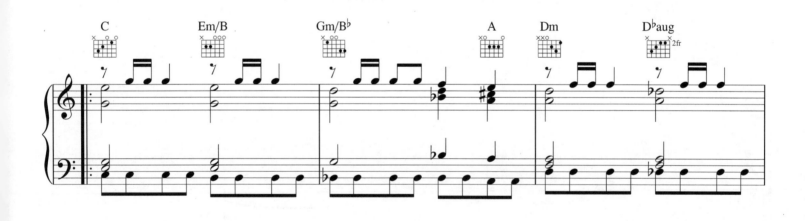

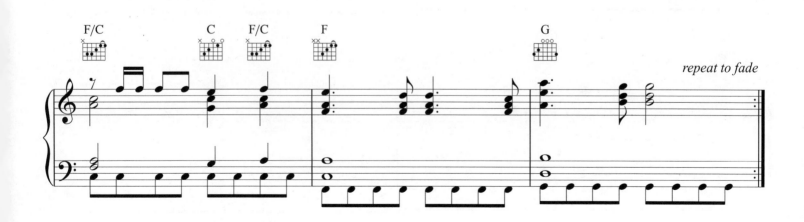

Missing

Words by Tracey Thorn
Music by Ben Watt

like the des-erts miss___ the rain.___

I step off___ the train,___ I'm

walk-ing down___ your street___ a-gain, past___ your door,___

I guess you don't live___ there an-y-more. It's

177

Keep The Faith

Words & Music by Jon Bon Jovi, Richie Sambora & Desmond Child

Yeah,   yeah,   yeah.

Guitar solo ad lib.

Play 3 times

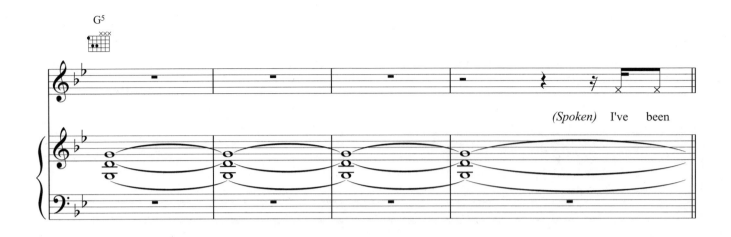

(Spoken) I've been

walk - in' in the foot - steps   of so - ci - e - ty's lies,   I don't

like what I see no more.   Some - times I wish I was blind,___   some -

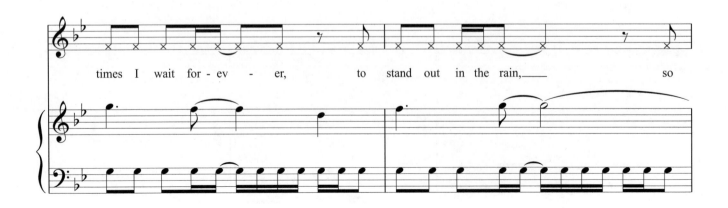

times I wait for - ev - er,   to stand out in the rain,___   so

184

Verse 2:
Tell me baby, when I hurt you
Do you keep it all inside?
Do you tell me all's forgiven
Or just hide behind your pride?

Everybody needs somebody to love
(Mother, father)
Everybody needs somebody to hate
(Please believe me)
Everybody's bitchin' 'cause the times are tough
Well it's hard to be strong when there's no one to dream on.

Faith, you know you're gonna live through the rain
Lord, we've gotta keep the faith.
Faith, don't you know it's never too late
Right now we've gotta keep the faith.

D.%.
Mother, father, there's things I can't erase
(Everybody needs somebody to love)
Every night we fall from grace
(Everybody needs somebody to hate)
Hard with the world in your face
(Everybody's bitchin' 'cause they can't get enough)
Try to hold on, try to hold on
(Everybody please, everybody keep the faith).

Strong Enough

Words & Music by David Baerwald, Sheryl Crow, Bill Bottrell, Kevin Gilbert, Brian MacLeod & David Ricketts

Married With Children

Words & Music by Noel Gallagher

There's no need for you to say you're sor - ry, good -

bye I'm com - ing home._____

I don't care_ no more so

To Coda

don't you wor - ry, good - bye, I'm go - ing home.____

1. I hate the way that ev - en though you know__ you're wrong, you say you're right.____
(Verse 2 see block lyric)

— I hate the books you read and all your friends,____ your

mu - sic's shite,____ it keeps me up all night, up all night.

Verse 2:
I hate the way that you are so sarcastic
And you're not very bright.
You think that everything you've done's fantastic,
Your music's shite, it keeps me up all night, up all night.

Shakermaker

Words & Music by Noel Gallagher

like to be some-bo-dy else and not know where I've been

(Verse 2 & 4 see block lyric)

I'd like to build my self__ a house__

out of pla-sti cine, ah, Ah,_____

_____ shake a long with me.

To Coda

Ah,_____ shake a long ____ with me. ____

I'm

sor - ry but I just don't know_____ I

know you said I told you so,____ but when you're happy and you're feel - ing fine____

198

Verse 2:

I've been driving in my car
With my friend Sister Soft
Mister Clean and Mister Ben
Are living in my loft.

Verse 4:

Mistetr Shifter sold me songs
When I was just sixteen.
Now he stops at traffic lights
But only when they're green.

Supersonic

Words & Music by Noel Gallagher

-ter-fall,__ no-bo-dy can see him, no - bo-dy can ev-er hear him call,

no - bo-dy can ev - er hear him call.

Verse 2:

You need to be yourself,
You can't be no-one else.
I know a girl called Elsa
She's into Alka Seltzer
She sniffs it through a cane
On a supersonic train.

And she makes me laugh,
I gor her autograph.
She's done it with a doctor
On a helicopter.
She's sniffing in her tissue
Selling the Big Issue

And she finds out ...

Take A Bow

Words & Music by Madonna Ciccone & Babyface

Moderate calypso feel ♩ = 80

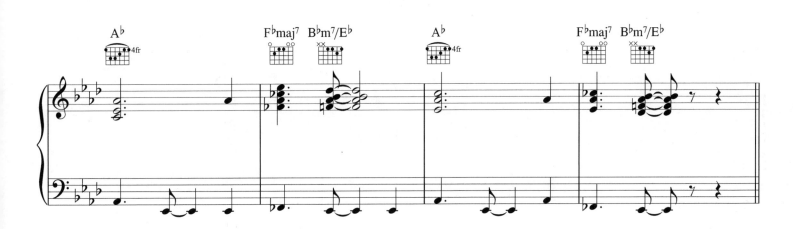

You took my love for grant- ed, why oh____ why. The show is o - ver say good-

1.
- bye. Say_____ good- bye._____

F♭maj7   B♭m7/E♭   2.4. A♭
Say good- bye.____   - bye.   I've al - ways been in love with

D.S.

209

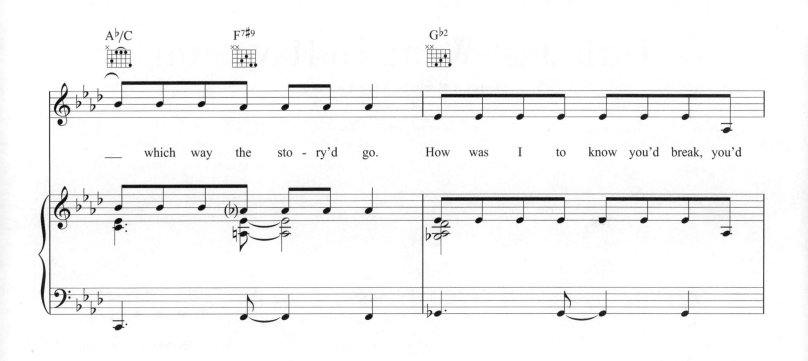

which way the sto-ry'd go. How was I to know you'd break, you'd

break, you'd break, you'd break, you'd break my heart?_____

D.S. al Coda
(vocal ad lib.)

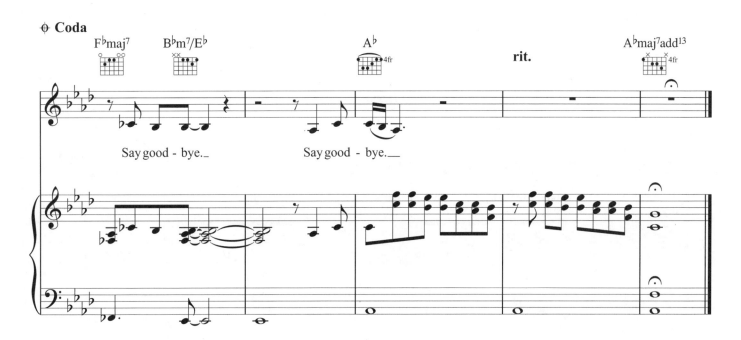

Say good - bye._ Say good - bye._

Girls Just Want To Have Fun

Words & Music by Robert Hazard

I come up in the morn - ing light,___ my moth-
The phone rings in the mid - dle of the night,___ my bud -

- er says when___ you gon - na live your life right?
- dy asks___ what you gon - na do with your life?

Oh ma - ma dear___ we're not the for - tu - nate ones, and
Oh dad - dy dear___ you know you're still num - ber one, but

girls___ they want to have fun, woah_ girls_ they want to have...

That's all they real - ly want

some fun _____ when the work - ing day_

_ is done,_ you know girls, they want to have fun. _____ Oh come on ___

rest of the world, I wan-na be___ the one___ to

walk in___ the sun.___

Hey now,___ hey now,___ what's the mat-ter with you, girls just___ want to have___

fun now.___ Hey now,___ hey now,___ what's the mat-ter with you,

Rock 'n' Roll Star

Words & Music by Noel Gallagher

To - night_____ I'm a rock 'n' roll

star.

To - night__

I'm a rock 'n' roll_____

star.

You're not down___ with who

Cast No Shadow

Words & Music by Noel Gallagher

walks a - long the o - pen road of love and life, sur - viv - ing if he can.

Bound with all the weight of all the words he tried to say,

chained to all the pla - ces that he ne - ver wished to stay.

they stole his pride.

As they took his soul they stole his pride.

As he faced the sun he cast

no sha - dow.

Road Rage

Words & Music by Mark Roberts, Cerys Matthews, Aled Richards, Paul Jones & Owen Powell

1. If all you've got to do____ to-day____ is find____ piece of mind,____ come 'round, you____ can take a piece of mine.____

And____ if all you've got to do____ to-day__ is____ hes-i-tate,__

Champagne Supernova

Words & Music by Noel Gallagher

slide,_____ in a cham - pagne su - per - no - va. a

cham - pagne su - per - no - va in the sky_____

1. Wake up the dawn and ask_ her why_ a
(Verse 2 see block lyric)

dream - er dreams she ne - ver dies,___ wipe that tear a - way_ now from your eyes

slide,____ in a cham - pagne su - per - no - va a cham - pagne su - per - no - va. 'Cause

peo - ple be - lieve that they're gon - na get a - way for the sum -

- mer but you and I____ we live and die____ the

world's still spin - ning round, we don't know why, why, why,__ why, why.

How ma - ny spe - cial peo - ple change_ how ma - ny lives are liv - ing strange,_

Verse 2:
How many special people change
How many lives are living strange
Where were you when we were getting high?
Slowly walking down the hall
Faster than a cannon ball
Where were you while we were getting high?

Hey Now!

Words & Music by Noel Gallagher

1.3. I hitched a ride with my soul by the
(Verse 2 see block lyric)

side of the road,＿＿＿ just as the sky＿＿＿ turned black.＿＿＿

'cause time's_ no   chain,___   feel_ no   shame.___

2. The

251

Verse 2:
The first thing I saw
As I walked through the door
Was a sign on the wall that read
It said you might never know
That I want you to know
What's written inside of your head

And time as it stands
Won't be held in my hands
Or living inside of my skin
And as it fell from the sky
I asked myself why
Can I never let anyone in?

She's Electric

Words & Music by Noel Gallagher

1. She's e-lec-tric, she's in a fa-mi-ly full___ of ec-cen-

(Verse 2 see block lyric)

Can I be e-lec-tric too? Ah_____ ah.

Play 3 times

Verse 2:
She's got a brother
We don't get on with one another
But I quite fancy her mother
And I think that she likes me
She's got a cousin
In fact she's got 'bout a dozen
She's got one in the oven
But it's nothing to do with me.

257

Morning Glory

Words & Music by Noel Gallagher

1. All your dreams___ are made___ when you're chained to the mir - ror with your
(Verse 2 see block lyric)

ra - zor blade.___ To - day's the day___ that all___ the world___ will see___

need a lit - tle time to wake__ up wake__ up, need a lit - tle time to wake__

__ up, need a lit - tle time to rest__ your mind,__ you

know you should so I guess__ you might as well.__

What's the sto - ry morn - ing glo - ry, well__

you need a lit-tle time to wake__ up, wake__ up,

well,_____ what's the sto-ry morn-

-ing glo-ry, well,_____ you

need a lit-tle time to wake__ up, wake__ up.

well,

what's the sto - ry morn - ing glo - ry,

well,

you need a lit - tle time to wake

Verse 2:
All your dreams are made
When you're chained to the mirror with your razor blade
Today's the day that all the world will see
Another sunny afternoon
I'm walking to the sound of my favourite tune
Tomorrow doesn't know what it doesn't know too soon.

Some Might Say

Words & Music by Noel Gallagher

1. Some might say___ that sun-shine fol-lows thun - der

(Verse 2 see block lyric)

go and tell___ it to___ the man___ who can - not shine.___

Some might say___ that

a bright - er____ day._____ 'Cause I've been

stand - ing at the sta - tion, in need of e - du - ca - tion in the

rain_____ You

made no pre - pa - ra - tion for my re - pu - ta - tion once a -

267

Verse 2:
Some might say they don't believe in heaven
Go and tell it to the man who lives in hell
Some might say you get what you've been given
If you don't get yours I won't get mine as well.

Wonderwall

Words & Music by Noel Gallagher

To - day is gon - na be the day that they're gon - na throw it back to you,___

by now you should-'ve some - how re - al - ised what you got - ta do.___

may - be_____ you're gon - na be the one that

saves me_____ you're gon - na be the one that

Say You'll Be There

Words & Music by Eliot Kennedy, Jon B, Victoria Adams, Melanie Brown, Emma Bunton, Melanie Chisholm & Geri Halliwell

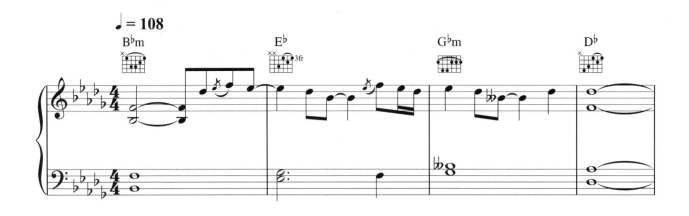

Oh say you'll be

there, I'm giv-ing you ev- 'ry-thing all that joy___ can bring_ this I swear._

1. Last time that we had this con-ver-sa-tion

I de-ci-ded we should be friends,_____ yeah. But now we're

go-ing round in cir-cles tell me will this dé-jà vu nev-er end._____ Oh

now you tell me that you've fall-en in love_ well I nev - er ev - er thought that would be,

(Verses 2 & 3 see block lyric)

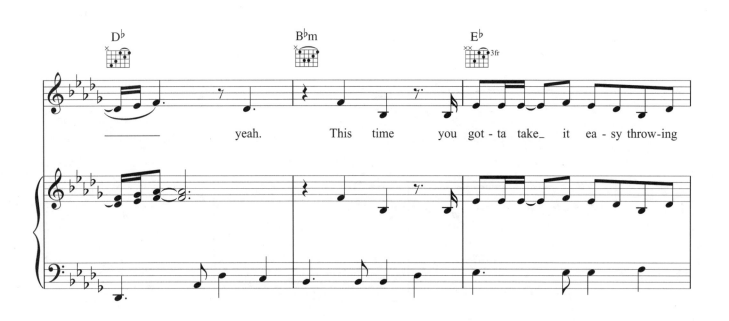

_____ yeah. This time you got-ta take_ it ea-sy throw-ing

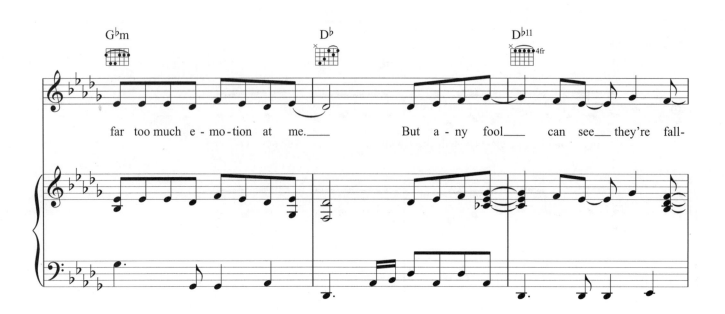

far too much e-mo-tion at me.___ But a-ny fool___ can see___ they're fall-

-ing, I got-ta make you un-der-stand. _____ (I'll)

I'm giv-ing you ev - 'ry-thing _ all that joy _ can bring, this I swear. _

_____ And all that I want _ from you _ is a pro-

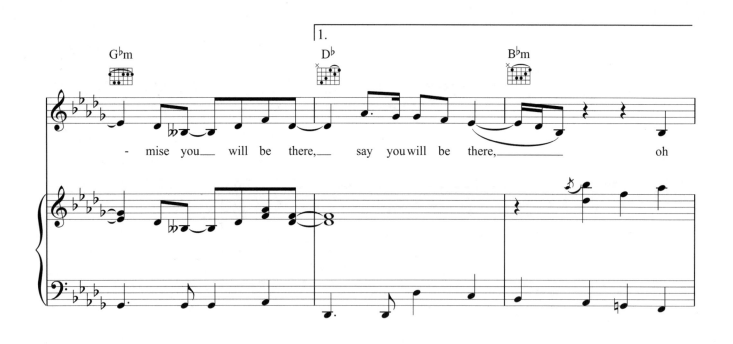

- mise you___ will be there,___ say you will be there,_____ oh

say you will be there, won't you sing___ it with me.___ ___

⊕ Coda

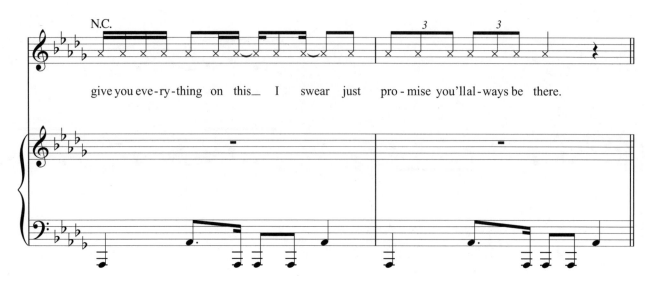

give you eve-ry-thing on this___ I swear just pro-mise you'll al-ways be there.

Verse 2
If you put two and two together you will see what our friendship is for,
If you can't work this equation then I guess I'll have to show you the door,
There is no need to say you love me it would be better left unsaid.

I'm giving you everything, all that joy can bring this I swear,
And all that I want from you is a promise you will be there,
Yeah I want you.

Verse 3 (Instrumental)
Any fool can see they're falling, gotta make you understand.

281

All Around The World

Words & Music by Noel Gallagher

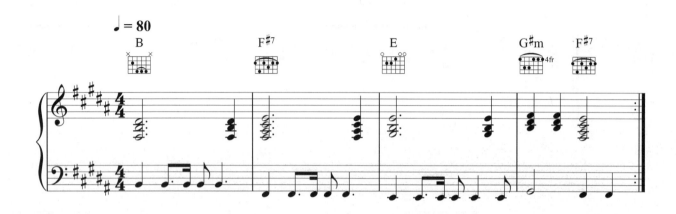

1. It's a bit ear-ly in the mid-night hour for me___ to
(Verse 2 see block lyric)

go through all___ the things that I want to be.___

290

Verse 2:
What you gonna do when the walls come falling down
You never move, you never make a sound
Where you gonna swim with the riches that you found
If you're lost at sea, well I hope that you've drowned.

Take me away *etc.*

Frozen

Words & Music by Madonna & Patrick Leonard

Moderately ♩ = 102

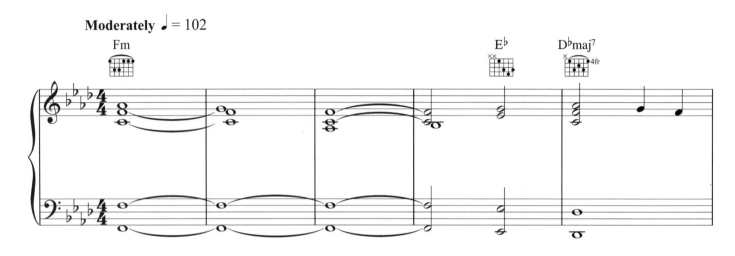

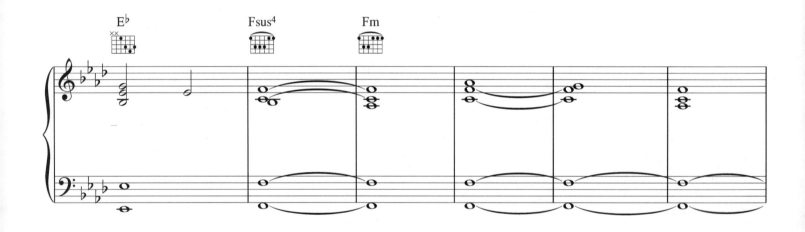

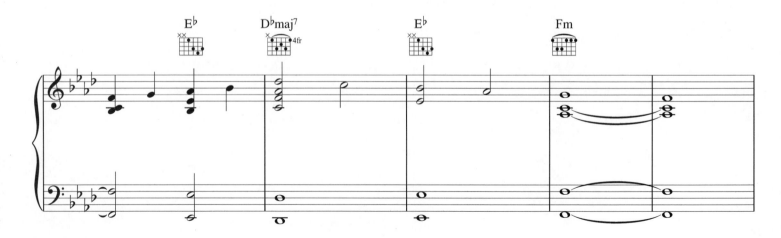

the key.   If   I   could melt   your___ heart.

Writing To Reach You

Words & Music by Fran Healy

301

The World Is Not Enough

Words by Don Black
Music by David Arnold

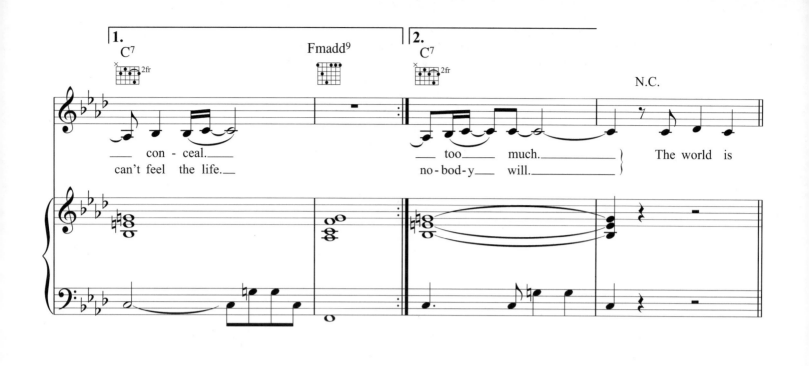

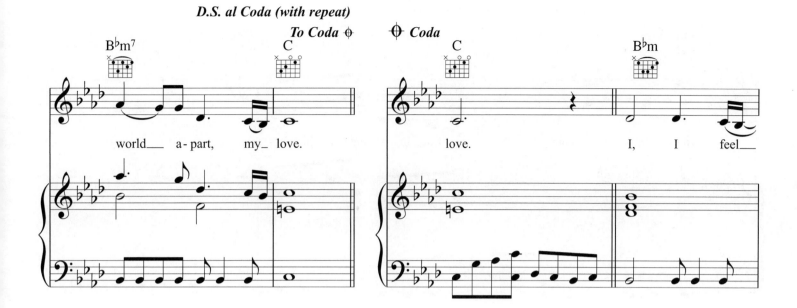

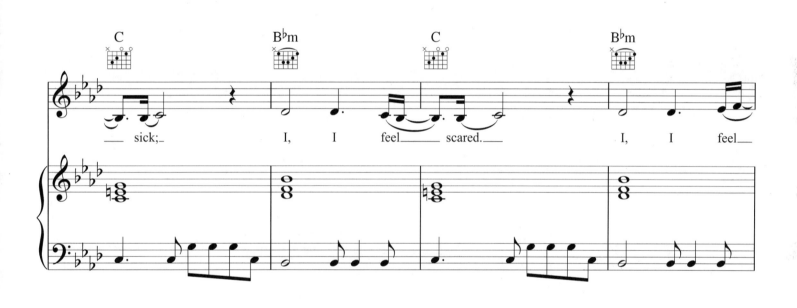

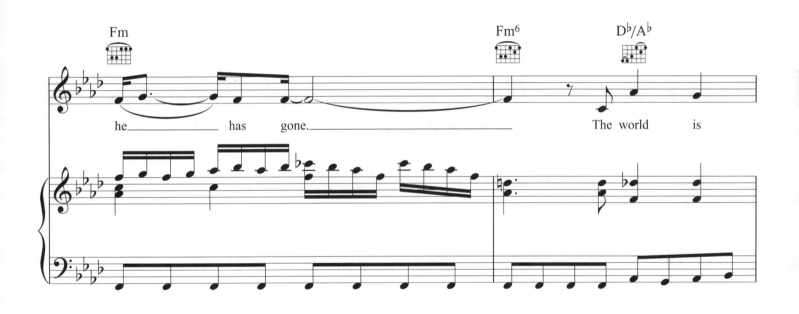

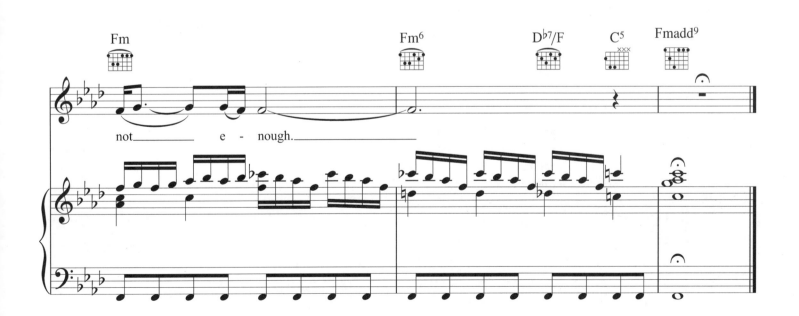

Why Does It Always Rain On Me?

Words & Music by Fran Healy

Verse 2:
I can't stand myself
I'm being held up by invisible men.
Still life on a shelf when
I got my mind on something else.
Sunny days, where have you gone?
I get the strangest feeling you belong.

Why does it always rain on me *etc.*

Verse 3:
As verse 1

Sing

Words & Music by Fran Healy

Verse 2:
Colder, crying over your shoulder
Hold her, tell her everything's gonna be fine
Surely you've been going too early,
Hury, 'cause no-one's gonna be stopped now, now, now, now, now.

Not if you sing *etc.*

Other Side Of The World

Words & Music by KT Tunstall & Martin Terefe

If You're Not The One

Words & Music by Daniel Bedingfield

Little By Little

Words & Music by Noel Gallagher

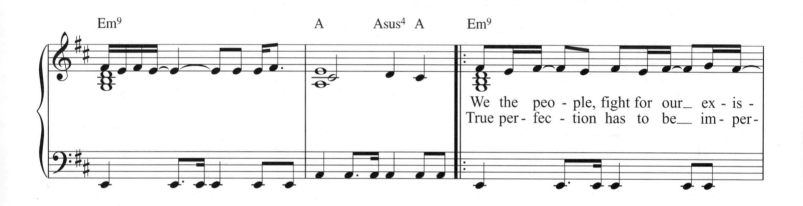

We the peo - ple, fight for our__ ex - is -
True per - fec - tion has to be__ im - per-

- tance.   We don't claim to be per - fect but we're
- fect.   I know that____ sounds__ fool - ish but it's__

free.   We dream our dreams a - lone_ with no__ re - sis - tance,
true.   The day has come and_ now you'll have to ac - cept the

Born To Try

Words & Music by Delta Goodrem & Audius Mtawarira

and all I tru - ly be - lieve_____ That I was born to try_____

I've learned to love_____ be un - der - stand - ing_____

___ and be - lieve in life_____ but you've got to make choi - ces_____

be wrong or right_____ Some times you've got___ to sac - ri - fice

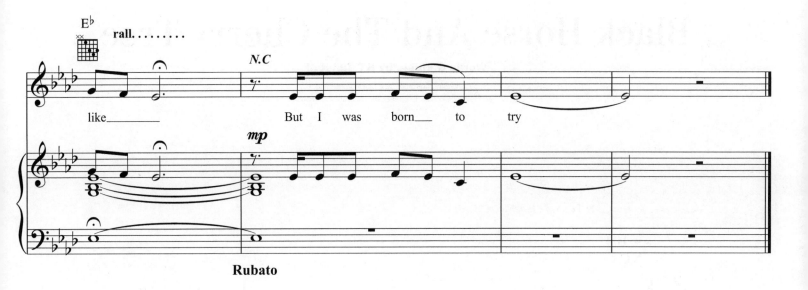

like_____ But I was born___ to try

Rubato

Verse 2
No point in talking what should have been
And regretting the things that went on
Life's full of mistakes, destinys and fates
Remove the clouds look at the bigger picture no - ooh

Black Horse And The Cherry Tree

Words & Music by KT Tunstall

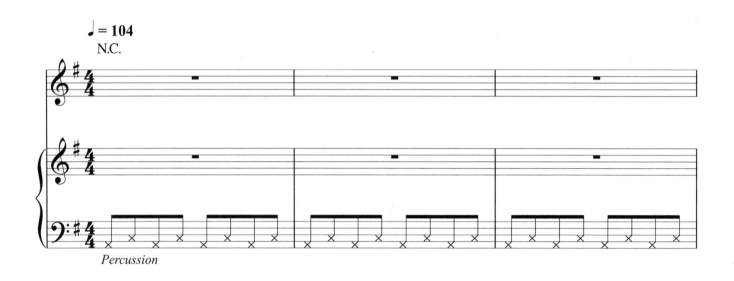

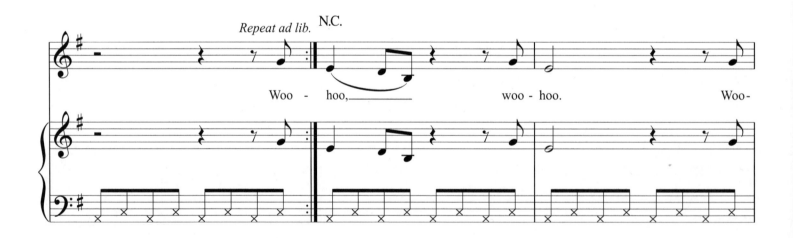

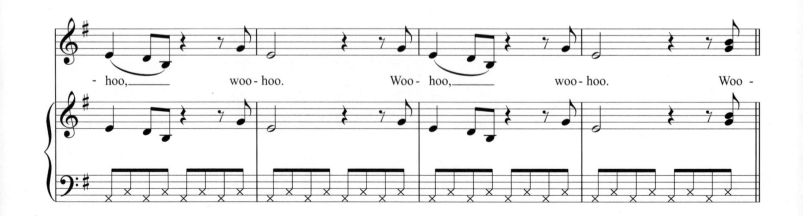

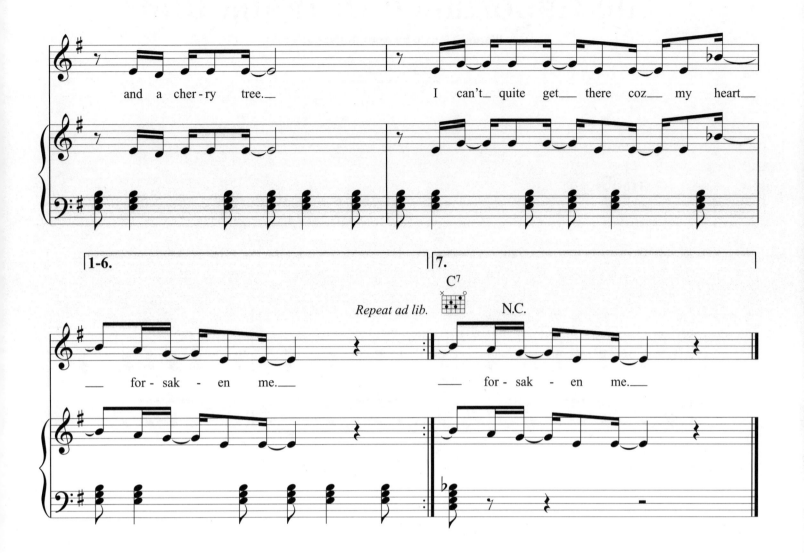

Verse 3:

And my heart hit a problem in the early hours
So I stopped it dead for a beat or two
But I cut some cord and I shouldn't have done it
And it won't forgive me after all these years.

Verse 4:

So I sent her to a place in the middle of nowhere
With a big black horse and a cherry tree
It won't come back, coz it's oh so happy
And now I've got a hole for the world to see.

The Importance Of Being Idle

Words & Music by Noel Gallagher

You Give Me Something

Words & Music by James Morrison & Eg White

Umbrella

Words & Music by Christopher Stewart, Terius Nash, Shawn Carter & Thaddis Harrell

Spoken: Uh-huh uh-huh, yeah, Rihanna. Uh-huh uh-huh, good

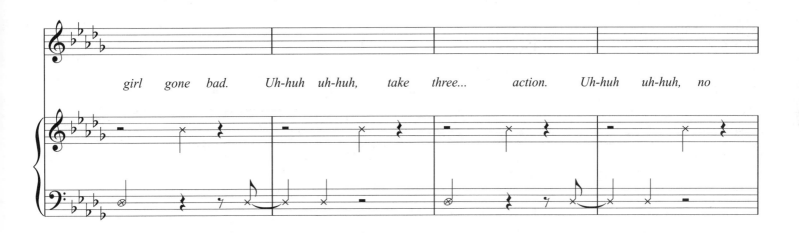

girl gone bad. Uh-huh uh-huh, take three... action. Uh-huh uh-huh, no

Eh eh eh,

clouds in my storms, let it rain, I hydroplane into fame, comin' down with the Dow Jones. When the

Repeat ad lib. and fade

361

The City

Words & Music by Ed Sheeran & Jake Gosling

the lights that blind   keep me a - wake._____
ful - fils my needs   and gives me com-pan-y when I need it.

Hood   up   and lace un - tied,_____   sleep   fills   my   mind.
Voic - es   speak through my   walls,____   I don't think I'm gonna make it

Can't   con - trol   what I'm in - to._____
past   to - mor - row._____

367

Halo

Words & Music by Ryan Tedder, Beyoncé Knowles & Evan Bogart

371

Love Story

Words & Music by Taylor Swift

Moderately

We were both young when

I first saw _ you. I close my eyes _ and the flash-back starts. _ I'm stand-in'

This love is dif - fi - cult, but it's __ real. __ Don't be a - fraid. We'll

make it out of this mess. It's a love sto - ry. __ Ba - by, just say __ yes."

Poker Face

Words & Music by Stefani Germanotta & Nadir Khayat

I wan - na hold 'em like they do in Tex - as plays:
I wan - na roll with him, a hard pair we will be.

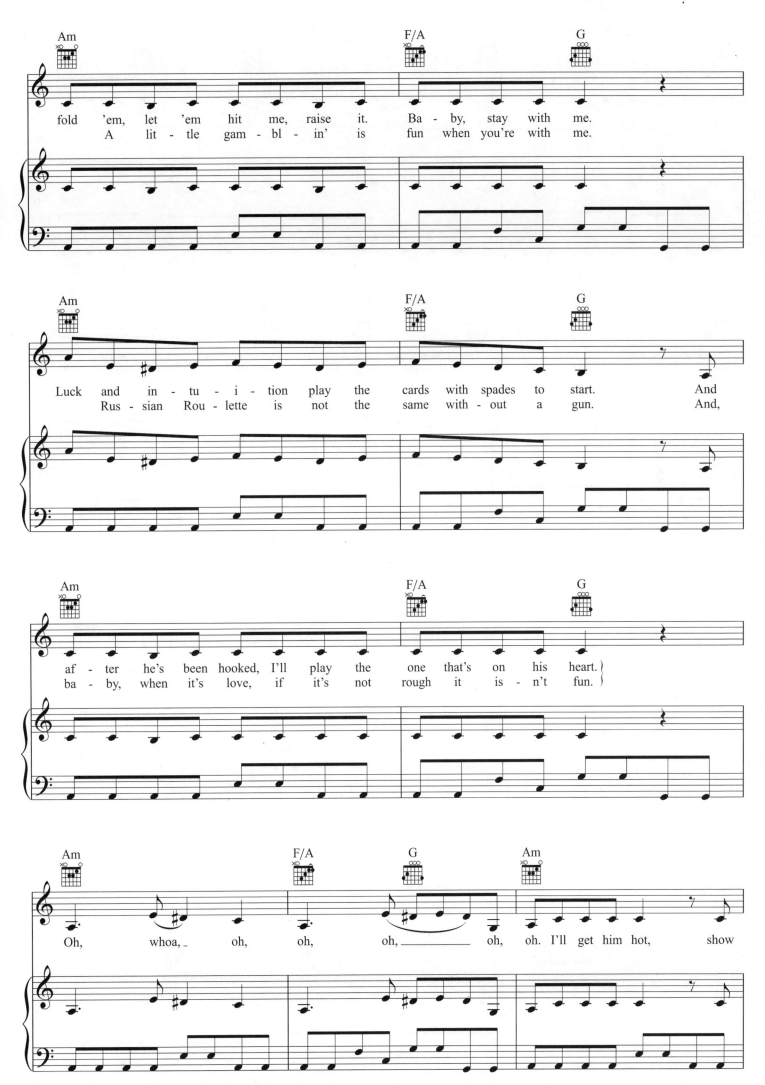

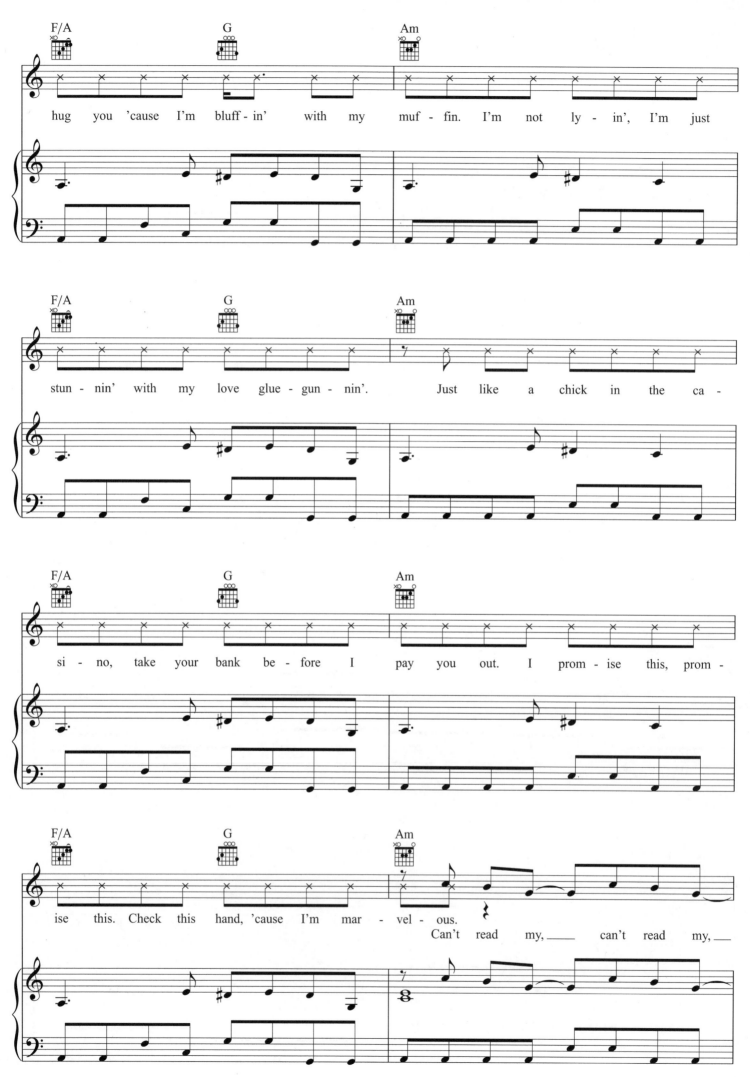

Suddenly I See

Words & Music by KT Tunstall

I can see her eyes look-ing from a page in a ma-ga-
-zine. She makes me feel like I could be a
tow-er. Big strong tow-er, yeah. The pow-er to be,
the pow-er to give, the pow-er to see, yeah, yeah. (Sud-den-ly I

Fight For This Love

Words & Music by Steve Kipner, Wayne Wilkins & Andre Merritt

The A Team

Words & Music by Ed Sheeran

Everything At Once

Words & Music by Lenka

411

Writing's On The Wall

Words & Music by Benjamin Drew, Eric Appapoulay, Richard Cassell & Tom Goss

1. We used to have fun,_____ now all we do is fight._
2. We used to talk,_____ now all we do is shout,

___ oh yeah. We know some-thing's wrong._____ It's
Our heads full of thoughts_____

417

ba - by,___ yeah.___ We both know it's a waste of time.___ Things___

ain't ev - er gon - na change. Oh,___ ooh.___

Oh, they ain't

gon - na change.___ Oh,___ no,___

no.

We ain't o-ver but the wri-ting's on___ the wall.___

We'll keep try-ing just so___ we can say___ we gave it all.___ We ain't o-ver but the

wri-ting's on___ the wall.___ This time next year we'll be no___ more.___

419

Drunk

Words & Music by Ed Sheeran & Jake Gosling

love.

All____ by____ my - self,____ I'm here a - gain.

All____ by____ my - self,____ you know I'll nev - er change.

All____ by____ my - self,____

Grade 8

Words & Music by Ed Sheeran, Robert Conlon & Sukhdeep Uppal

strum-ming on my heart strings like you were a grade 8, but I've nev-er felt this way. I'll pick your feet_

_ up off of the ground and nev-er, ev-er let you down, now. You're

strum-ming on my heart strings like you were a grade 8, but I nev-er felt this way. I'll pick your feet_

_ up off of the ground and nev-er, ev-er let you down, now.

To Coda

Hold my heart to stop me bleed - ing_ now, now, now,

and I'll nev - er let_ you down._ Hold my heart to stop me bleed - ing_ now,

now, now, I'll nev - er let_ you down._ *2° (You're)*

strum-ming on my heart strings like you were a grade 8, but I've nev - er felt this way. I'll pick your feet_

Marry The Night

Words & Music by Fernando Garibay & Stefani Germanotta

soldier to my own emptiness, I'm a winner. I'm gonna marry the night.

I'm gonna marry the night. I'm gonna marry the night.

I'm gonna marry (Marry.) the night. (The night.)

I'm not gonna cry anymore. I'm gonna marry the night. Leave

437

439

Price Tag

Words & Music by Lukasz Gottwald, Claude Kelly, Bobby Ray Simmons & Jessica Cornish

this man, you can't put a price on the life. We do this for the love so we fight and sac-ri-fice ev-'ry

night. So we ain't gon stum-ble and fall nev-er, nah. Wait-

-ing to see this in the sign of de-feat, uh - uh. So

we gon' keep ev-'ry one mov-ing their feet. So bring

back the beat and then ev-'ry-one sing. It's not a-bout the

mon-ey, mon-ey, mon-ey.__ We don't need your mon-ey, mon-ey, mon-ey.__ We just wan-na make the

world dance,__ for-get a-bout the price tag.____ Ain't a-bout the

(Uh.) cha-ching_ cha-ching. Ain't a-bout the (Yeah.) b-bling,_ b-bling. Wan-na make the

This

Words & Music by Ed Sheeran & Gordon Mills

Video Games

Words & Music by Elizabeth Grant & Justin Parker

1. Swing-ing in the back-yard. Pull up in your fast car,
2. Sing-ing in the old bars. Swing-ing with the old stars.

whis - tl - ing my name.
Liv - ing for the fame.

O - pen up a beer and you say get o - ver here and play a
Kiss - in' in the blue dark. Play - in' pool and wild darts,

do.___ (Now you do.) (Now you do.) (Now you do.) Now you do.___

___ (Now, now you do.) (Now you do.) (Now you do.)___

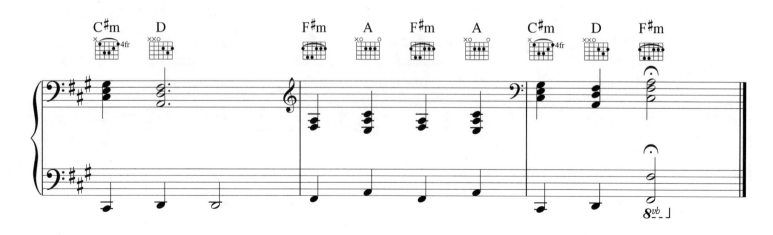

Wings

Words & Music by Mischke Butler, Michelle Lewis, Thomas Barnes, Peter Kelleher, Benjamin Kohn, Iain James, Erika Nuri, Jessica Nelson, Jade Thirlwall, Heidi Rojas, Perrie Edwards, Leigh-Anne Pinnock, Christopher Dotson & Kyle Coleman

459

Let Her Go

Words & Music by Michael Rosenberg

love her when you let her go.

On - ly know__ you've been

high when you're feel-ing low.

On - ly hate the road when you're miss -in' home.__

On - ly know you

love her when you let her go.

And you let her go.___

464

Dear Darlin'

Words & Music by James Eliot, Edward Drewett & Oliver Murs

tried.   Been think-

Bm   A

-ing   a - bout the bar__ we drank__ in.   Feel-ing like the so - fa was sink-

Em   Bm

-ing.__   I was warm   in the hope of your eyes.   So if my

G   Gmaj7   A

words break through the wall   and meet you   at your door,   all I can say is

Little Things

Words & Music by Ed Sheeran & Fiona Bevan

1. Your hand fits in mine like it's made___ just for me. But
2. I know you've nev-er___ loved the crin-kles by your eyes when you smile.___

We Are Never Ever Getting Back Together

Words & Music by Max Martin, Taylor Swift & Shellback

*Vocal 8vb till ***

1. I re-mem-ber when we broke up the first time, say-ing "This is it I've had e-nough." 'Cause, like, we

had-n't seen each oth-er in a month when you said you need-ed space. What?

Then you come a-round a-gain and say "Ba-by, I miss you and I swear I'm gon-na change, trust me." Re-
(2.) real-ly gon-na miss you pick-ing fights and me fall-ing for it, scream-ing that I'm right and you would

-mem-ber how that last-ed for a day? I say "I hate you." We break up. You call me. "I love you."
hide a-way and find your peace of mind with some in-die re-cord that's much cool-er than mine.

Ooh._____ We called it off a-gain__ last night.__ But
Ooh._____ You called me up a-gain__ to-night.__ But

479

481

22

Words & Music by Taylor Swift, Max Martin & Johan Schuster

I don't know a-bout you, but I'm feel-in' twen-ty - two.____

Ev-'ry-thing will be al-right if you keep me next to you.____

You don't know a-bout me, but I'll bet you want____ to.____

Ev-'ry-thing will be al-right if we just keep danc-in' like we're

489

Get Lucky

Words & Music by Thomas Bangalter, Pharrell Williams, Guy-Manuel de Homem-Christo & Nile Rodgers

1. Like the leg-end of __ the
2. The pre-sent has __ no

493

Let Me Go

Words & Music by Gary Barlow

loved. So this is gon-na take_ a bit of get-ting used_ to, but I know what's

right for you.

Fly

high_____ and let me go.

That

sky_____ will save your soul.

When you pass__ by,_____ then you'll
know that this is gon-na take__ a bit of
get-ting used__ to, but I know what's right for you. Let me__
go. you. Fly

D.S. al Coda ⊕ *Coda*

501

Little Talks

Words & Music by Ragnar Thorhallsson & Nanna Bryndis Hilmarsdottir

Ghost

Words & Music by Ryan Tedder, Noel Zancanella & Ella Henderson

Give up the ghost.___ Give up the ghost.___ Give up the ghost._

Stop the haunt-ing ba — by. Give up the ghost.___ Give up the ghost.___

— Give up the ghost.__ No more haunt-ing ba — by.___

___ I keep go-ing to the riv-er.___

I'm A Mess

Words & Music by Ed Sheeran

_____ it out,_____ how._____ Go-ing through the mo-
_____ this feel-ing now._____ We're go-ing through the mo-

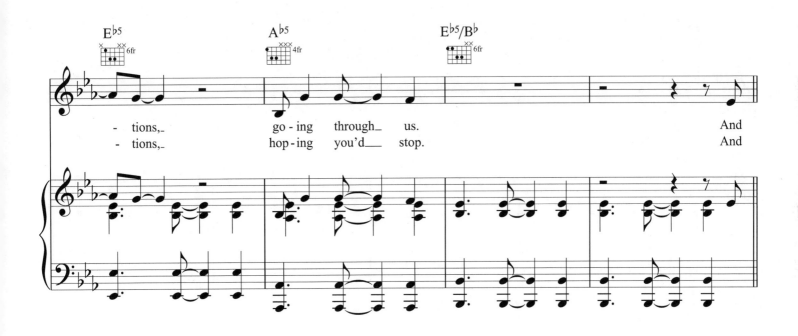

- tions,_ go-ing through_ us. And
- tions,_ hop-ing you'd_ stop. And

oh I've_____ known_____ it for the long-est time,_____ and all of my hopes,_____
oh I've_____ on - ly caused you pain_____ I know,_____ but all of my words

525

I'm Not The Only One

Words & Music by James Napier & Sam Smith

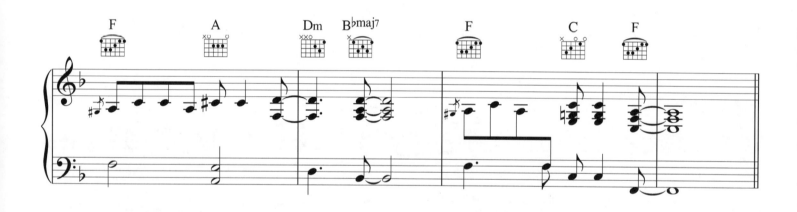

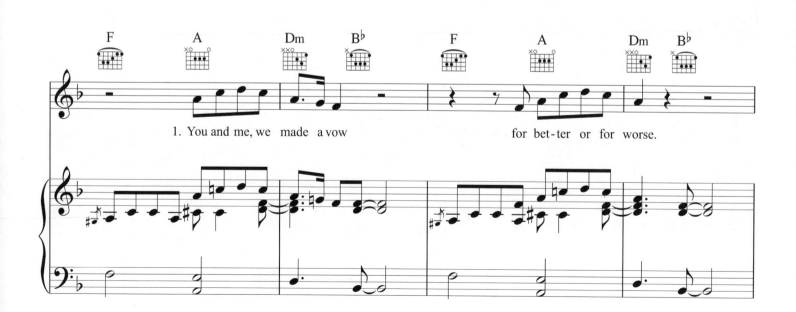

1. You and me, we made a vow   for bet-ter or for worse.

One

Words & Music by Ed Sheeran

535

Nina

Words & Music by Ed Sheeran, John McDaid, Jermaine Scott, Jay Hippolyte & Isra Lohata

Rather Be

Words & Music by James Napier, Grace Chatto, Jack Patterson & Nicole Marshall

As long as I am with___ you,
As long as we're to - geth - er   there's

my heart___ con - tin - ues___ to beat.___
no place I'd rath - er___ be.___

With ev - 'ry step we take,   Ky - o - to to the Bay.   Stroll - ing___ so ca - sual - ly.___

We're dif - f'rent and the same,   get you a - noth - er name.

Stay With Me

Words & Music by Tom Petty, Jeff Lynne, James Napier, Sam Smith & William Phillips

1. Guess it's true I'm not good at a one night stand.
2. Why am I so e-mo-tion - al?

But I still need love 'cause I'm just a man.___
No, it's not a good look, gain some self con - trol.___

stay___ with me?___ 'Cause you're___ all___ I need.___ This ain't_

___ love, it's clear___ to___ see. But darl - ing stay_____ with me._

Coda

D.S. al Coda

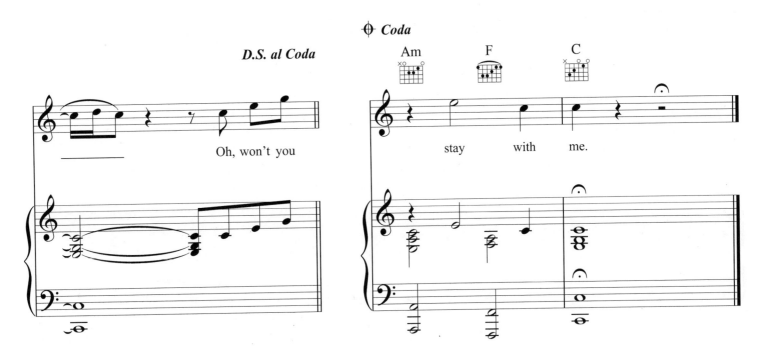

Oh, won't you   stay   with   me.

Take It Back

Words & Music by Ed Sheeran & John McDaid

us._____ Don't you fade in-to the back, love. No._____

Mhm..._____

Verse 3:

And take it back now.
Now, I don't ever wanna be perfect.
'Cause I'm a singer that you never wanna see shirtless.
And I accept the fact that someone's got to win worst-dressed.
Taken my first steps into the scene, giving me focus,
Putting on a brave face, like Timothy Dalton.
Considering a name change, thinking it was hopeless.
Rhyming over recordings, avoiding tradition.
'Cause every day's a lyric and the melody can be written.
Now absence can make your heart ache,
But drinking absinthe can change your mind-state, vividly.
Need to let my liver be. And I'll say it again:
Living life on the edge with a close handful of friends
It's good advice from the man that took his life on the road with me.
And I hope to see him blowing up globally
'Cause that's how it's supposed to be. I'm screaming out vocally.
It might seem totally impossible, achieving life's dreams.
But I just write schemes.
I'm never having a stylist, giving me tight jeans.
Madison Square Garden is where I might be.
But more likely you find me in the back room of a dive bar with my mates.
Having a pint of McDaid discussing records we made.
And every single second knowing that we'll never betray the way we were raised,
Remembering our background, sat down.
That's how we plan it out. It's time to take it back now.